The Early Belle Epoque Corset

1890
Worth
Court Gown

Plate 1

1891
Worth
Caftan Gown

1892
Worth
Dust Cloak for Motoring

Plate 2

1893
Worth
Evening Gown

1894
(Probably Creed)
Bicycle Dress

Plate 3

1895
Worth
Dinner Gown

1896
Rouff
Walking Costume

Plate 4

1897
Révillon
Calling Costume

1898
Félix
Resort Costume

Plate 5

1899
Dickins & Jones
Bathing Attire

1900
Paquin
Dinner Gown

Plate 6

1901
Beer
Ball Gown

1902
Doeuillet
Opera Cloak

Plate 7

1903
Raudnitz
Dinner Gown

1904
Walles
Walking Costume

Plate 8

1905
Martial & Armand
Afternoon Dress

1906
Drecoll
Summer Town Dress

Plate 9

The New 1908 Corset

1907
Matilde Sée
Winter Town Dress

Plate 10

1908
Paquin
Evening Gown

1909
Buzenet
Evening Gown & Cloak

Plate 11

Plate 12

1910
Lelong
Tailored Suit

1911
Agnes
Visiting Dress

1912
Lanvin
At Home Dress

1913
Boué Soeurs
Picture Dress

Plate 13

1914
Laferrière
Ball Gown

Ca. 1915
Fortuny
Gown & Cape

Plate 14

1916
Lucille
Evening Dress

1917
Worth
Suit

Plate 15

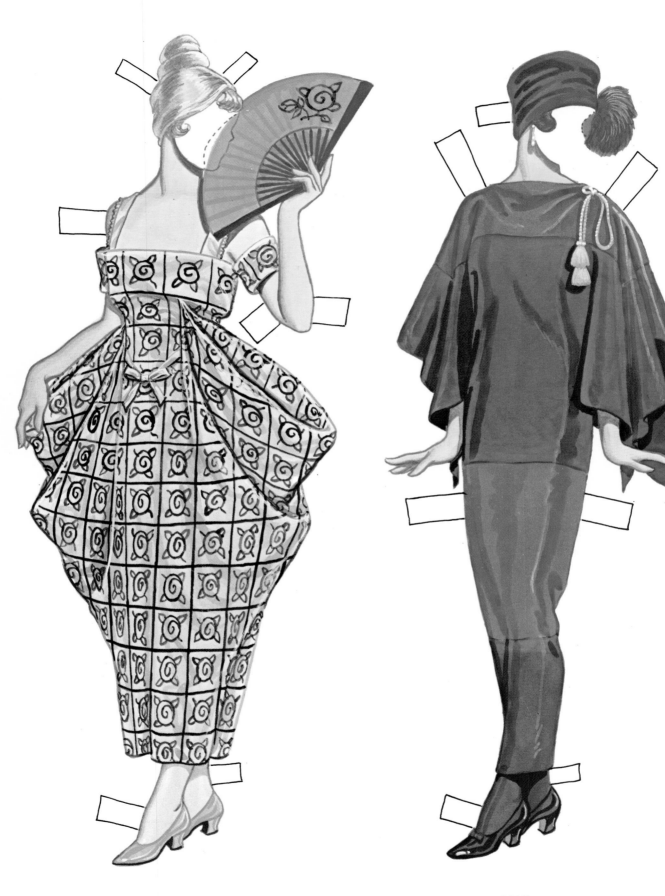

1918
Doeuillet
Evening Gown

1919
Poiret
Dinner Gown

Plate 16